A Poet I Am Not

Seryca Monroe

Presentation by *BookLeaf Publishing*

Web: www.bookleafpub.com

E-mail: info@bookleafpub.com

ISBN: 9789357440837

First edition 2023

*To my friend JD, who leaves me notes.
You've never stopped believing in me, and I
hope you know how much I appreciate you.*

ACKNOWLEDGEMENT

Thank you to Bookleaf Publishing for making it possible to publish my first book—wow, I can't believe that's true!
Also thank you to all my favorite poets for giving me some inspiration.

"You can feel the poetry rotting in your stomach."

—Mary Ruefle

PREFACE

I am not a poet.
A poet I am not.

I Was Raised

By a tam wearing
regalia owning
hair like a peacock's feather looking woman
Technically

By transitional phrases
and lead-ins
lowercases
and random caPitaliZatiONS
that pave my way
to hireaths I find between pages
Actually

By a blood red book of dares to D and L
an "I didn't fall in love with you, I flew" by M
a diary of repeated and crossed out "I am not
insane" from J
and a double used "Arrange whatever pieces
may come your way"
Practically

By "One. Two. Two-and-a-half. Three."
"The need for speed"
"So was Red"
and "L-I-V-I-N"

Certainly

By "Sandra Templeton, I love you"
"In Omnia Paratus"
"You're tacky and I hate you"
"Sanka, you dead man?"
and "This one time at band camp"
Really

By bold posters screaming to SMASH THE
PATRIARCHY!
because equality is a hierarchy
and my body is no man's property
Surely

By fictional worlds
First and last chapters
Takes one and one hundred
Quotes no one recognizes
Wandering within world I never wish to leave
And drowning in my non-existent tears from
when it all ends
Truly

I was raised
by fEmiNists and FictIoN
Basically

Interlude

Things are getting closer
My adolescence is fading in and out
They say pride is the devil but then
why am I not six feet underground?

I'm getting deja vu from you
but I don't think I can see it through
As a matter fact my life just feels like an
interlude

Now kid, the climb back ain't so easy
there ain't no role models here
Except maybe your neighbors
The lost ones are all near

We're the false prophets
The immortal lovers
The forbidden fruit nobody wants to take a bite

And in the morning
when we've been high for hours
Four your eyes only
everybody dies

This land of the snakes

is crumbling
And the "american dream"
is tumbling

Nobody told me growing up that everyone in
this world is a prude
But now I know it to be true
And I can't help but feel like this is all some sick
ol' interlude

A Wonderland State of Mind

I fear I'm just as daffy as the Cheshire Cat
And mad as Mr. Hatter
Suppose I could get loopy with Alice and never
see the matter
Maybe in the homeland of the cooky I could
have some freedom to sing with the flowers and
paint the roses red and blow out rings from my
mouth of A's, B's and C's.
Suffice it to say I would much rather be between
the pages of Lewis Carroll's mind right now
I think Wonderland would be a fun break

Ars Longa, Vits Breva//Art is Long, Life is Short

Mirum est quod dum spiro, spero
Spes mea ad ultimum
Suus 'iustus atramento in charta quamquam
Quid ergo dico?
Si autem dies unus iustus deficiet

Ars longa, vita brevis
Forsitan eam servare possum in pagina
Sed cum littera durat, quid atramento accidit?
Exsiccatur et marcescit?
An verbum scriptum ardet?
An imbre diluit?
Sic in sepulchrum convertetur?//Wonderful to
say that while I breathe, I hope
Hope for my word to last
It's just ink to paper though
So what do I say?
If it will one day just fade away

Art is long, life is short
Maybe I can keep it on a page
But when the letter lasts, what happens to the
ink?

Does it dry up and fade?
Or does the written word burn?
Does it wash away with rain?
So in its grave it will turn?

the falling of icarus and me

there is a poem i've forgotten about icarus
something about him laughing, for there is a sort
of "bitter triumph in crashing when you should
be soaring"
and my goodness, could you imagine?
arms spread as you plummet
laughing at the world doomed to be against you
flying against all odds, only to be kissed by
death and burned by dripping golden terror
no wonder icarus laughed
i would too
forget about the inevitable and impending catch,
to get all you've ever wanted, if even just for a
moment
there is a terrifying beauty in burning when you
should be glowing

Don't (Repition poem)

I've heard it for as long as I can remember. I've
heard it since I wore a short dress.
I've heard it since I got boobs and wore a tank
top.
I've heard it since I started wearing makeup.
I've heard it since I started high school.
I've heard it since I saw that girl on the news get
hurt by those men.
I hear it everyday.
I'm used to it by now
Which is why I don't get angry anymore.
"Don't wear that, you look like a ho."
"Don't wear that, you look stuck up."
"Don't wear that much makeup, you look like
you belong in the corner of the street."
"Don't look so tired, put on some makeup."
Don't—
Don't—
Don't—
Don't—
I'm not angry anymore. It makes my chest hurt
though, and not wear boys stare.
It makes my heart burn, because this isn't for
you.
I didn't put on makeup for your pleasure.

I didn't put on a short dress so that your dick will get hard.
I shouldn't have to cover my shoulders.
Boys just need to learn to keep it in their pants.

A note from a friend

I tell an everlasting tale
My faith was in a breeze
A wandering wish was my dream
I chase time but it is ever so a fleeting memory
I wish for only to understand and know agony
The meadow I till everyday
So come by
At least in the dreams you may perceive
I digress my case

Another note from a friend

If you are alone, I will always be there
I am nothing but you are something
So just know I will be the shoulder you can cry
on always
If you cannot live on then live for me
Remember I too once felt that way
Relieved only by my dreams
I needed a crutch to keep me stable
Let me be that for you

One more note from a friend

Sometimes a person's first flowers are when they're dead. Don't let that be you.

to the crazies who giggle

there is beauty in death. i read once that beauty
is terror, and that in its purest form, beauty is
quite distressing. but so is death. there are few of
us who giggle at funerals and smile at the reaper,
but those who do are the ones that see the
terrible beauty. they see the defiance in life. they
buy a bouquet of flowers for their lovers, but
take out the wilted ones to keep for themselves.
they know what that flower feels like and revel
in the relation. if you giggle at funerals, i think
you're the ones who truly know what beauty is.
you're the beautiful ones yourself.

you pick me and i prick you

i am a rose in a garden full of daisies
i can't be tend to without drawing blood
so everyone left me alone
until you came and saw my thorns and smiled
you always liked a challenge

pink.peonies.and.your.lips.

there.was.a.night.i.went.to.pick.peonies.for.my.h
air.and.the.sky.was.as.pink.as.the.peonies.in.the.f
ield.and.the.peonies.were.pink.as.your.lips.when
.we.kissed.and.i.think.i.never.truly.loved.the.colo
r.pink.until.that.night.

Sapiosexual: One who is attracted to the intelligence of another

Touch me with your words and I will shake
Find the poems inside of me and I will quake
Tell me what quotes turn you on and I will recite
them until you gasp
We'll tell each other beautiful words until our
voices are but a rasp
Fuck me with your mind
Draw me in and let me be worth your time
Let me drown in the vocabulary of your body
and let me lick your thoughts whole heartedly
Go down on my intelligence
Thrust deep into the folds of my wits until I
cannot think
And let's be flustered together

That's it

When my thoughts frown, you make them smile.
That's it. That's the poem.

When he calls me beautiful

i am ugly.
everyone knows it.
so do i.
but.
for some reason.
he thinks i am beautiful.
and that makes me feel beautiful.
what a funny thing it does to my heart when he
says it.

Greedy

Your eyes are a poem and each stanza is better
than the last

Your touch is a story and I want you to keep
writing it

Your lips are a song, please let me keep listening

Your hair is a cloud and I want to run my fingers
through it

You're poetry and stories and songs and skies
and I want to read and listen and see you

You are everywhere and in everything and I
want it all

Fears

They asked me what I was scared of most.
I said falling in love.
"Why?"
"For two reasons. People often fall out of love
for the same reason they fell. I think it's sad that
something someone once found beauty in about
you is what they now find ugly. I don't want to
be a piece of poetry just for you to burn the
page."
"What's the other reason?"
"I don't believe in love."

A universe of pain

You made stars out of my scars and then
constellations out of those you looked at me like
I look at the moon but made me feel as warm as
the sun when you talked to me it was like we
were in another planet and you told me you
loved me from here to the galaxies far far away
... it's to bad you left me with a black hole ...

Ten times

Ten times I called
Ten times you didn't pick up
Ten times I dialed your number
Ten times I stopped when the feeling got to
rough
Ten times I just wanted to hear your voice
Ten times I thought I annoyed you
Ten times I knew I wasn't your first choice
Ten times I texted
Ten times you left me on read
Ten times I decided leaving you alone would be
better instead
Ten times you could've just told me to leave you
alone
Ten times you made me feel like shit inside of
my own home
Ten times I wish you would just tell me why
Ten times I cry falling asleep at night

Song titles in CAPS

WHEN I MET YOU I was the type of
KISSAPHOBIC girl
that was FALLING FOR THE VILLAIN
But THE NIGHT WE MET, it felt like I could
breathe. It was like THE FIRST DAY OF MY
LIFE

My CLICHÉ THOUGHTS took over and I was
a TEENAGER IN LOVE wrapped in CUPID'S
CHOKEHOLD

We did a STALKERS TANGO and SPARKS
flew
We were OUT LIKE A LIGHT in seconds from
an electric feeling
Thursday I don't know if I LIKE OR LIKE
LIKE
But FRIDAY I'M IN LOVE and that I am sure
of

It was a HAPPY LIFE when we were together,
and that is true
Maybe it was wrong, but I wanted you to BE
MY MISTAKE
And that's exactly what it was

A BEAUTIFUL MISTAKE
But that is what first love is, right?
Corruption of the finest kind

Dear future me

I hate everything around me and I can't make it
better
Maybe I should forget about it or I could write a
letter
To myself addressed in five years time
Or maybe ten
It would say something silly like:
Dear future me,
Hey how have you been?

I hope you graduated with honors just like we'd
always hoped for
I hope you got into our dream college the one
we saw on that tour
I hope it treated you well and that you're back
for some more
I hope you got that job we always wanted and
that it's treating you well too
I hope you found a really great guy that takes
you to art museums for dates and holds you
instead of asking why? When you cry

And most of all Dear future me,
I hope you found somewhere new that you can
call a home

Away from this place we always dreamed of
leaving
And when the tears rush down your face and
your chest is heaving
at least you know you're not alone

Dear future me,
Things are getting crazy back here
and all I can do is sit and stare
at the chaos surrounding mostly in my head but
some of it's out there
But you knew that already, didn't you?
I try to let my guard down
though I fear no one wants to be around me that
long
But I don't shed a tear because I know I'm not
alone
And thank God I have you
But this letter is growing long
So I must bid adue